Younger Spotter's Guides

WILD FLOWERS

Su Swallow

Illustrated by Hilary Burn
Designed by Sally Burrough
and Niki Overy
Edited by Sue Jacquemier and
Jim Roberts

This book shows some of the more common wild flowers that grow in Britain. Some of them may grow in your garden. Others grow in fields or woods, or along hedgerows. You should also look on waste ground and along roadsides.

The flowers in this book are arranged by colour to make it easy to look them up. Some flowers look alike so check the leaf shapes to make sure you have found the right name. The fruits or seeds may also help you to name the plant.

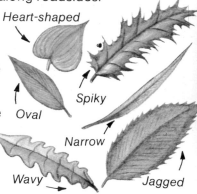

Heart-shaped

Spiky

Oval

Narrow

Wavy

Jagged

Only pick wild flowers if there are a lot of the same kind growing together. Never dig up a wild plant by the roots. Many wild flowers have become rare because people collected them.

If you find a flower that is not in this book you could draw it in a notebook and look it up later in other books.

Take a notebook and pencils

When you spot one of the flowers in this book, make a tick in the box under its picture.

A dandelion "clock"

Dandelion

Dandelions grow in grassy places. The yellow flowers close up at night. You can blow away the seeds from a dandelion "clock". There is a white juice in the stalks.

Celandine

This small plant has shiny, heart-shaped leaves. The petals are shiny yellow and pointed. Look for them in the spring in woods and damp, shady places.

Buttercup

Look for the shiny yellow
Buttercup flowers in the
summer. The leaves are
hairy and have jagged
edges. Buttercups grow in
grassy places.

Cowslip

The small yellow Cowslip
flowers grow in little
bunches. The leaves grow
round the bottom of the
stalks. Look for them in the
spring, in grassy fields.

Primrose

Primroses grow in woods
and fields, and by hedges.
They flower in the spring,
and sometimes in the
winter too. Primrose leaves
look like Cowslip leaves.

A seed pod

Bird's Foot Trefoil

This plant grows in grassy places. It is called Bird's Foot Trefoil because the seed pods look like birds' claws. Look for the yellow flowers in the summer.

Wild Pansy

The Wild Pansy is smaller than garden pansies. It flowers from the spring to the autumn. The flowers are violet or yellow, or both. Look for it in grassy places.

9

Flower
buds

*The flowers
look like this*

Forget-me-Not

Forget-me-Not leaves feel
soft and hairy. The tiny
flower buds are pink, but
they turn blue when they
open. The Forget-me-Not
grows in open places.

Violet

Look for this small plant in woods in the spring. The flowers have no smell. The leaves are heart-shaped and grow in a clump. The flowers have five petals.

Speedwell

Large patches of Speedwell
grow in grassy places and
woods. The blue flowers
open in the summer. Each
flower has four tiny petals.

Bluebell

Bluebell flowers are bell-shaped and have a sweet smell. They grow in shady woods and spread out like big blue carpets. You can see them in the spring.

A rose hip

Dog Rose

The Dog Rose climbs over hedges and can grow very tall. It has sharp thorns, and pink or white flowers. In autumn and winter birds eat the red rose hips.

The flowers and fruits look like this

Cow Parsley

Some people call this plant Lady's Lace. Several other plants may look the same, so check the leaves, flowers and fruit. It grows in hedges and flowers in the spring.

Blackberry

This plant climbs up hedges.
It has prickly stems and
leaves. In the autumn, when
the berries ripen and turn
black, they are good to eat.

A flower bud

Bindweed

Bindweed has pink or white flowers, shaped like trumpets. Look for them in the summer in waste places. The twisting stems climb up walls and hedges.

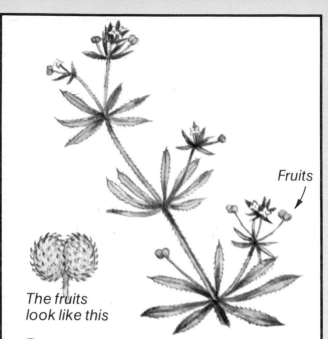

Fruits

The fruits look like this

Goosegrass

Goosegrass climbs over hedges. It is covered in tiny hooks so it sticks to clothes and animals' fur. The tiny white flowers come out in the summer.

Berries

Black Nightshade

This weed grows in gardens and fields, and on rubbish tips. Its white petals fold back. The black berries are poisonous, so do not touch them.

White Deadnettle

This plant looks like the Nettle, but the hairs on its leaves do not sting. The flowers grow in clusters around the stem. Look in hedges and waste places.

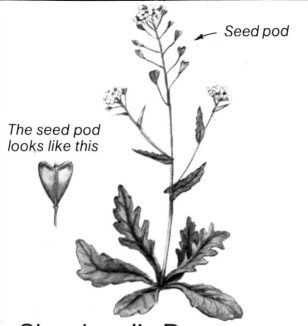

Seed pod

The seed pod looks like this

Shepherd's Purse

This plant grows on waysides and in waste places. It is also a common weed in gardens. You can see the flowers and seed pods all the year round.

Chickweed

You can see Chickweed
flowers all through the year.
It is a common weed in
fields and gardens. It grows
quickly and can soon cover
big patches of ground.

The main stem is called a runner

White Clover

Farmers often grow Clover to feed to their animals. It also grows wild on garden lawns and in fields. Notice how the main stem grows sideways along the ground.

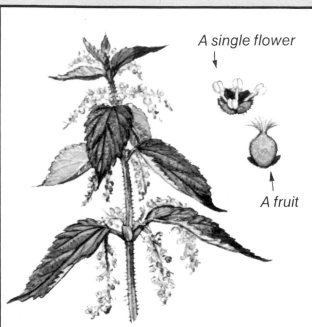

A single flower

A fruit

Nettle

The tiny hairs on Nettle
leaves sting if you touch
them. The flowers are green
and hang down. Nettles are
common on waste land, in
gardens and on roadsides.

Daisy

Daisies flower from spring to
late autumn. The flowers
close at night and in bad
weather. The leaves grow at
the bottom of the plant.
Daisies grow in short grass.

Plantain

This low plant grows well in
places where people walk.
You will find it on paths and
lawns, and on waste ground.
The tiny flowers grow in
spikes in the summer.

Knapweed

Knapweed flowers look like little pink brushes. They grow on stiff, hairy stems. Knapweed grows in grassy places and flowers in the summer.

Foxglove

Look for Foxgloves in woods in the summer. They grow quite tall. Their flowers are trumpet-shaped and are purple or white. Bees crawl inside them.

The flowers look like this

Heather

Heather grows as tough
little bushes. It has tiny
leaves, and spikes of pink or
white flowers. Look for it in
the summer, on heaths and
moors.

A flower bud

A seed pod

Poppy

It is easy to spot Poppies in cornfields and on waste ground. Their flowers are bright red and silky, on hairy stems. Look for them in the summer.

A seed pod

Red Campion

Look for this bright pink
flower in early summer, in
woods. Notice how the
leaves grow in pairs up the
stem. The stem is hairy and
sticky.

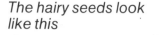

The hairy seeds look like this

Rosebay Willowherb

Some people call this plant Fireweed because it often grows on bonfire sites and other burnt ground. The hairy seeds are blown away by the wind.